SWALLOWING STONES

SWALLOWING STONES

Carole Coates

Shoestring Press

All rights reserved. No part of this work covered by the copyright hereon may be reproduced or used in any means – graphic, electronic, or mechanical, including copying, recording, taping, or information storage and retrieval systems – without written permission of the publisher.

Printed by imprintdigital
Upton Pyne, Exeter
www.imprintdigital.net

Typeset by narrator
www.narrator.me.uk
enquiries@narrator.me.uk

Published by Shoestring Press
19 Devonshire Avenue, Beeston, Nottingham, NG9 1BS
(0115) 925 1827
www.shoestringpress.co.uk

First published 2012
© Copyright: Carole Coates
The moral right of the author has been asserted.

ISBN 978 1 907356 53 7

ACKNOWLEDGEMENTS

With acknowledgements to *The Rialto, Other Poetry, ShadowTrain*.

EDITOR'S NOTE

Kor has only entered Western European writing twice before. Rider Haggard is responsible for most of the myths about Kor but there are some aspects of his novel *She* (1887), that correspond to the facts of the country. The geography of *She* is reasonably factual as are the lost city, the statue and the Amahaggar tribe. However, Haggard has Kor in entirely the wrong continent; his descriptions of the city and statue make them sound very late Victorian and it goes without saying that in Kor there is no all-powerful goddess-like woman who has lived for two thousand years and can kill with a touch of her finger.

Elizabeth Bowen, in her short story *Mysterious Kor* (1944), evokes the beauty and strangeness of the lost city as it appears in the dreams of a young woman experiencing the London blitz. Bowen's wartime stories are rightly celebrated for their other-worldly quality and the lost city of Kor is an excellent metaphor for this. Both the Haggard novel and the Bowen short story are recommended reading.

It is now old-fashioned to refer to "Kor", as, like Mumbai, it has reverted to its own spelling. It became Czurr in 2005. But as these texts were written before then, it was thought more appropriate to retain the old European spelling.

*I believe the soul
is a kind of swallowed stone*

Jean Sprackland, "Soulless", *Hard Water*, 2003

CONTENTS

The poems are a series of monologues voiced by either visitors to Kor or by Kor residents. Among the visitors are Frank Changeling, a British academic in 1980; Femke Romkema, wife to Eelco, an engineer on the diamond fields in 1980; Charles Harding, a TV archaeologist in 1998 and Barbara Wells, a recently elected New Labour MP in 1998.

The Kor residents voiced here are Lena Falada; her niece Anna; her nephews Ren and Fil and her brother Jon Falada, a farmer. The Falada farm is situated in the remote Kamiros province near the ancient and abandoned ruins of Kor Old City. Other Korish voices include two Priest-Guardians and a Seminary Police Chief.

These characters are entirely imaginary.

Prologue, 1960	1
Vertical Zonation, 1960	3
Song before Birth, 1960	5
PART ONE, 1980 – 1983	7
Letter to Molly, 1980	9
In the Holy House	12
Letter to Molly (2)	14
Letter to Molly (3)	16
Lena at Falada Farm, Kamiros	19
Letter to Molly (4)	22
The House of the Perfects	23
Swallowing Stones	25
PART TWO, 1990 – 1998	26
Boys are like diamonds, girls are like cotton	29
My First Visit to the Salt Room	31
Where Have You Gone?	33
Grace before the Meal	35

Nameless	37
Mud Flowers	38
Fil	40
The Job of Apprehending Dark Spirits	43
Tiptoe	46
In the bar of the Kor New City Meridian Hotel	47
The Gabriel Christ	50
The Angel Rendezvous	54
At the Ministry	60
In Praise of Ruins	63
Butcher	66
Up Country	67
Patriarch	70
Ghost	72
Ancient Kor	75
The Dancing Girl	78
What She Said	81

In memory

*Nadia Anjuman
1980 - 2005*

Prologue, 1960

VERTICAL ZONATION, 1960

> Extract from an after-dinner speech given to the Highgate Rotary Club by Professor Marcus Willett-Roberts (University of London), 10 January, 1960, on the subject *Alexander Von Humboldt: Great Geographer.*

Another of Von Humboldt's bright ideas,
though not as useful as the isotherm,
was mapping climate zones by altitude.
He showed how one could climb from tropical
to micro-thermal, or even higher up
to permanent ice and snow. This, gentlemen, is called
altitudinal zoning. The Andes are a good example.
Another one is that remote place — Kor.
If you can get there, it's a paradise
for geographers. The coast is marsh, sub-tropical,
lagoons, mosquitoes, mud: the flood plain
of the laziest river. Water hardly moves.
But follow it upstream to higher ground,
the climate changes. You're in orange groves.
Keep climbing, you'll soon walk in apple orchards
with a cool wind from the mountains.
Higher still, they're planting rye, potatoes.
(And gentlemen, you'll be pleased to hear
that ladies do this sort of thing in Kor!)
The mountains are great beasts
of fifteen thousand feet, then a sheer drop
to desert. Huge and hot as hell.
Only one cartographer got that far.
He never came back. Few maps of Kor
exist and none of the desert. As I said —
a geographer's dream. Von Humboldt would agree.
The desert, though unmapped, is not unnamed.
The Korish call it *Mind of God.*

And, gentlemen, the Rotary Club
has this in common with the Mind of God:
no women are allowed there.

SONG BEFORE BIRTH, 1960

Traditional song sung at the birth of Lena Falada

Midwife, midwife, bring us a boy *(sung by men*
We will give you honey cake *waiting in the*
We will give you pearls *Salt Room)*
Midwife, midwife, bring us a girl
We will give you kick on kick
We will give you tears.

Bring us a son as bright as a diamond *(sung by women*
Bring us a son as hard as a mountain. *downstairs)*

Take that mud grub, that pump slug *(men's voices)*
That sand worm, give her back to the ditches
Force her back down
To the slime and the weeds
Back to the frogspawn.
Give her back to the waters.

Otherwise *(women's voices)*
Otherwise
Otherwise

Black waters will rise *(men's voices)*
Up through your cellars
Creep up your stairs
Defile the Salt Room
Pollute to the stars.

So *(women's voices)*
So
So

Prologue, 1960

Bring us a son as strong as the desert   *(women's voices)*
Bring us a son as wise as salt.

Midwife, midwife, bring us a girl   *(men's voices)*
We will give you kick on kick
We will give you tears.
Midwife, midwife, bring us a boy
We will give you honey cake
We will give you pearls.

Part One, 1980 – 1983

Part One, 1980–1983

LETTER TO MOLLY, 1980

Letter from Frank Changeling to his wife, May 1980

My dear,

        I love your notion that being in Kor is like
watching a tennis match played with invisible balls.
Invisible to me at any rate. Gestures, I can see,
and movements — but what they relate to is opaque.
Maybe one day I'll see the ball. I tell myself this
after each long day studying the language.
I can talk to people now, not that they want me to,
often they walk away. Foreigners have been as rare as phoenixes,
(if you can use the plural) but soon will be like seagulls — everywhere.

They've already started on the new city. Yesterday,
with the greatest ceremony, but no bands or fireworks —
that's not the Korish way — the first building was opened.
You must imagine a bare plain above the river,
tractors instead of trees, churned up mud, uneven concrete paths
leading from villages that will become the suburbs of the city,
Aren where I'm lodging, Fend and Sidmar… I forget the other.

Obviously the first building is a church — huge as a Mormon
                                                  temple but octagonal
and on the steeple, not a weather vane but a crimson angel with
                                                  condor wingspan.
All courtesy of *Alberic, USA*. it says on the plaque by the door. Also
they provide the Art. That's what I want to tell you about.

The service (improbably they let me in) was reminiscent of the
                                                    Greek Orthodox
with lots of deep male chanting, priests and congregation like
                                                   great answering gongs.

I envied them. I could observe that oceanic feeling,
belonging to something bigger than oneself, but I fidgeted
like an awkward adolescent at a wedding.
Afterwards I stayed behind to look at the walls. Alone.
You'd think they'd make more fuss about wall panels by Moth.
(Remember when we saw his stuff in the Tate?)

At first I saw huge desolate rectangles,
dark entries that were sealed by layers and layers...
but I looked and looked and I was seeing not down
but up through water, fathoms of water, with sometimes dark expanses
and sometimes sharp oblongs of light. There's nothing, I think,
                                                            no, and then
miles away, no, years away, something suspended — high
                                                                  fragments maybe,
curves like ancient ropes or whorled shells or even whale ribs
and then rust-coloured spurs of something, mottled impasto... and
navy and prussian blue and sometimes lapis
and scraps of bronze foil dropping,
yellow and orange like rust-flowers, like lichen,
blue shadows of curved parallel lines.
I don't know what I saw — it was unfathomable,
sometimes turquoise green expanses and then gulfs of darkness
                                                                            rising up.
I can't explain it. Sometimes it seems I saw
some terrible fragments frozen in disintegration or maybe
it was something coming together very painfully and slowly,
waiting to coalesce.

                                                                  It was a space
so full of meaning I couldn't write yesterday night or study. I
                                                             watched the stars instead.
There's no pollution here — not yet at any rate — and they were
                                                                bright as diamonds.
Diamonds of course will make Kor's fortune (courtesy of
                                                            Alberic, USA).

Oh, I know where that tennis ball trope comes from — Arts
                              Cinema, Cambridge, 1967.
Antonioni's *Blow Up* and that ten shilling biryani we had afterwards.
God, what a long time ago, Molly, such ages and ages ago.

IN THE HOLY HOUSE

> Extract from The Sermon of the Salt-Flats, preached by Priest-Guardian Rickas at the Inauguration of the new Holy House, the first to be built in Kor New City on the first day of the Feast of the Return, 1st May 1980.

Welcome, brothers to the Holy House this holy day of The Return,
the blessed day our Seer came home to us, bringing
the One God of the Desert Books. Friends, think of this:
men dulled from the day's work, looking up to the hills
hearing a shout, a rattle of stones, seeing a flash of metal.
The Seer was coming with his gold, his horses, his disciples,
and alas, Mary, his wicked wife. Satan torment her.
A humble salt trader touched three times by God.
As it says in The Stone Book

God spoke to him first in the Salt-Flats
when he was a young man rising up before dawn
to load his donkeys. Think of that moment,
a man pure as salt, pure as the desert air
walking toward God. The sun rose,
the salt flats shone like a silver mirror
and God came in a crystal mist. The Seer,
appalled, fell down crying out *Which God are you?*
As it says in the Stone Book

We know God's gracious answer
I am the One God. There is none else.
You do wrong to worship trees and rivers
and household things. One God only
should you worship. Take your salt, load your donkeys,
travel further out through many deserts
until you find the place where I alone am God.

Learn and teach. You are the Seer.
As it says in the Stone Book.

Brothers, friends, what can we learn? First,
that God came as a mist of salt to the young Seer.
Destroyer, Preserver, He exalted the power of salt
so that we call it God's Sweat, keep it sacred in our houses
and we have left the idolatrous ways of the past,
enshrining willows and olive trees, the silly rituals of the river.
But you must still beware the paltry spattering of blossom,
gladness of seed in mud. The God of Salt is a serious God.
As it says in the Stone Book
As it says in the Stone Book
As it says in the Stone Book brought to us by the Seer.

LETTER TO MOLLY (2)

>Extract from a letter written by Frank Changeling to his wife, June 1980.

I'd heard there were nightingales. At least I thought that's what it said.
Those compound words can be misleading but the name of the village
means something like *the place where night birds gather to...*
and then a couple of syllables I can't make out
but must mean *sing*. What else do birds do after all?
It's known as Relin D. (So many Relins which simply mean *the place*.)

So I set out to find this Relin, seven miles away, and hear the
                                              nightingales.
(I wish that you were here to share my walks. I am so solitary.)
It was late afternoon but still hot walking between the maize fields.
A flat country here, so I could see the cloud of willows for a long time
ahead of me. I got there just as school was finishing —
which it did without any British zoo noise. Orderly quiet boys in
                                                single file,
each with a book under his right arm.

Relin D's a small place, built round the wooden church and
                                                schoolroom,
less than forty houses, but some quite sizeable and all of them
                                                traditional
with that outside staircase I told you about, ornate with folk
                                                emblems.
A few men leaned over the balustrades, cigarettes in their mouths.
Such a pity that most of the men have forgone native dress
to wear slacks, tee-shirts, jeans and gym shoes.
Luckily the women keep tradition. I watched them
coming in twos and threes into the square. (They've got
a modern pump and the old well is sadly neglected.)

I sat under the willows to watch the scene. The willows, I should say,
are a kind of hybrid — the height of the cricket bat willow
with long fronds of the weeping variety. They dabble the water
of a series of small ponds, populated by water-birds
of a serious disposition. Not as impressive as those swans at Stratford.
Do you remember how they surged up to strip young leaves
from the willow branches, leaping from the water?
I sat down by a pond and got my notebook out.
You must imagine the sun falling toward the fields
and women with pitchers, like a Bible story, dignified in their robes
and their hieratic face-wear. They moved slowly, going and returning
as if in some archaic place, gold-lit by the setting sun.
Even the tiny children had a classic air assuming
quaint and immemorial postures. But the women were
Arcadian Pastoral. Oh, they were performing, and quite
without realising, a slow dance to the music of time
itself. I was, as you can imagine, furiously taking notes.

The light went suddenly — night falls so quickly here —
just as I got to my Poussin comparison, but I had a torch
and waited for the nightingales. It was dark as pitch
as I ate my sandwich. Then I thought — is that a firefly?
And another one? Then further away, another? A dozen fireflies
glowing in the dark among those willow trees. Then one grew
                                                        brighter
and some one coughed. Smoke drifted on the pond and smelt of
                                                        nicotine.

I thought I'd leave the nightingales. Perhaps there weren't any.
Maybe *night birds* means owls. I didn't hear them either.
In fact, I heard no birds. All the way back through the dark fields
I heard only rustlings. Maybe they need a moon before they sing.

LETTER TO MOLLY (3)

Extract from letter written by Frank Changeling to his wife, July 1980.

Back in Oxpra now, Molly, the port I came to first
and where I bought those pearl and onyx beads (I hope you wear
them).
It's so much more cheerful than Aren, though I'm grateful to the
priest
for putting me up and teaching me the language. But there are
people here
who speak English and ask me out for a beer. And from my window
I can count thirty bright brass tea pots, all hung along the market wall.
There's a hubbub — a seemly sort of hubbub, this being Kor
and some delicious smells, one like frying toffee.
I thought I heard some laughter, even singing, but that's frowned
on in public
so Femke tells me. I've learned more from her
and her husband, Eelco, in the last few days than
in three months in Aren. Femke and Eelco Romkema
are Dutch (a Friesian name I think) and staying at the same hotel.
An engineer, he works in the diamond fields. We talk all night.

Last night, we drank Bessenjenever and Boomsmaberenburg
and got horribly honest. You would have enjoyed it, Molly.
You'd like Eelco and you might like Femke. This is the sort of
thing she says:

We should be silent like beetles, like earwigs. Words are lies.
Take Korish for example. 'Amahaggar'. Do you know that word?

Yes, I said, *doesn't it mean 'little helper' like an au pair?*

Wrong. The Amahaggar are a different ethnic group.
They live in the north and have for centuries and quite unwillingly

*provided slaves for Kor. They're bought and sold. So what
does 'Amahaggar' mean?*

Molly, that was the first I'd heard of it.
Slavery in Kor! *But they're so religious.*

You know the word for 'self' in Korish? — consciousness? she said
*'Ferethereg.' It's a compound word that means 'home of the soul"
or "resting place of the spirit". These people are so
full of soul, they can't attend to other things.*

It's hard for Femke here, Eelco said, *but Kor will improve
with diamond money.* She disagreed, while I maintained
that Kor should keep itself well away from the modern world
(although that slavery worried me). The Boomsmaberenburg
was finished and we were very drunk. Too drunk for bed.

As for me, I said, *now that I know the language* (Femke laughed)
I'm going to the mountains. I'll pick a guide up there who knows the sites.

*But first I'll show you my place, the diamond basin. It's something
to see, something to tell your kids.* Eelco was full of energy.
*It's what was left by the old open-cast mining — still impressive.
We're working on the pipe now down in the granite gneiss,
not in the basin, but come and look. Come now. It'll soon be light.*

Yes, I know, Molly, we were stinking drunk.
You would have stopped us. Femke went to bed.
But the road was empty and all the way Eelco was shouting
about quartzite and quartz porphyry and melaphyr.
It was still dark when we arrived. No moon.
Star-light and Eelco's torch and shadows blacker
than darkness. We danced and sang a bit and waited for the dawn.
When we stopped, I heard an echo underground.
I couldn't sing again. I was watching a great stain
on the ground that darkened as the sky greyed.

Eelco was asleep in the car but I stood very still —
it seemed for hours — as the light strengthened
and the stain on the ground seemed larger, huge, immense
until it wasn't a stain at all but a gigantic hole
still almost full of darkness. I stood there

among the stubby grass feet from the edge.
Molly, that pit slowly, slowly filled with light
and I could see the sheer grey and white walls, shining, smooth,
striated down and across like monochrome tartan,
the huge wheel and winding gear and deep,
deep below — viridian water.

It was a great inverted mountain of empty air
and I stood on its edge. One step forward or one back?
I shouldn't tell you this.
But of course, I woke up Eelco, started the car
and drove us back to Oxpra.

                    I shall pack tonight,
start out for Kamiros tomorrow.

LENA AT FALADA FARM, KAMIROS

Lena Falada, June 1980.

Young women are like the small red deer glimpsed in the Rego foothills.
Such creatures are shy and delicate but will come down
to the pools to drink and, later, feed from your hand.
The Stone Book, Verse 72.

If a woman open a book, that very moment her husband dies.
The Stone Book, Verse 79.

Nobody will marry me. I have too many secrets
and I walk in forbidden places.

I scrub the floor with my left fist
which is a sign of the devil

and sometimes I laugh too loud
at my own jokes in the square.

I have touched pitch and am reviled.
Reviled or defiled? I can't remember.

There's so much they don't know.
I should be like glass, clean glass

but I'm not. Instead I am here
locked in my room to repent yet again.

I count my steps from door to bed
Seven. And I count the flagstones

but I forget, lose count, finding dead things
in the white stones, patterns, pictures

and I think of my forbidden city
which is over there to the left behind the hill.

I want to be there with my outlawed things —
my three books and my notebook and the gold chain

I found in the room where the lady is.
I want to be there again to see her face

and sweep her floor and brush away the cobwebs.
Then I'll be happy to come back and work.

Two pictures on this wall —
good St Joseph in white

and Christ climbing up the blue sky.
How easy to do that, easy

to float away out of reach
ascending to a red cloud

which will bus him to heaven.
There are other ways to get there.

My mother thinks I should become
one of the Perfects. I refuse.

My brother's wife threatens me
with the rice farms in the wetlands.

So I prick a red bracelet
round my wrist and feel better.

Bright red beads on blue and white skin
on the brown ropes of other wounds.

The new-born baby is a girl.
They say they will keep her.

She'll be my job, though. Her mother
cares for her boys only.

How many choices for those thrown-away girls?
And how many choices for girls like me?

Nurse-maid, scrub-woman, care-taker,
gardener, wood-chopper, field-hand,

apple-picker, cook, salter of meat,
seamstress, bottler of fruit, lighter of fires,

knitter of wool, grower of herbs,
healer of wounds, washerwoman... .

LETTER TO MOLLY (4)

> Frank Changeling to his wife, September 1980

Molly, I must be quick.
I'll give this to Femke to post.
They'll search me at the airstrip,
confiscate the photos.

They're all I've got.
It's all wrong, it's all gone wrong.
Christ, Molly, I couldn't have known,
I couldn't have known.

Eelco's got me a seat on the flight.
If they let me out. If.
I can't stand any more jail
or those terrible Gabriel kids.

Femke is angry and says
What have they done with the girl?
Oh God, I don't know.
How can I know?

Take care of these photos
and notes — if they reach you.
I think I'll go mad if they don't.
Molly, I hope to see you soon.

THE HOUSE OF THE PERFECTS

> *Priests and commentators have objected to this term on the grounds that the women cannot with any certitude be classed as "Perfects"; preferring an altogether more cautious title such as "The place where young women, postulants, attempt perfection."*
> Dance, N., *Christian Cults*, New York, 1977, p.101.

Femke Romkema, October 1980

But the locals call it *The Pebble House*.

We would assume a well inside the courtyard and there is talk of
                                                                                      bushes —
a tangle of currant bushes whitening every spring but
no fruit softens on the branch. Are they white currants?
Or red? But they are hardly food, after all.

Sometimes hooligans or mothers fling figs or chocolate bars,
curfew-dodging silently, or sometimes one will shout
if the Gabriels are absent, but this is frowned on
and may result in conversations with the police.

Twenty years ago, folk came to see ropes hanging
down from each window (*sacred pigtails*, Ozen said
in his poem on the subject), ropes hacked back and back each month,
until the stumps were given to the families as relics.

These days, each female's weight is broadcast on TV
between the prayers and recipes and when one becomes Perfect
a priest will chant the verse all day on the Women's Channel
A stone will nourish if the appetite is holy* and a white bird is
                                                                          released in the Square.

*The Stone Book, Verse 175

The stones are smooth and round, found in mountain waterfalls
and brought to the city with great reverence. The first is given
when the woman discards her bleeding, the second when she dissolves
her breasts and the third when she grows a fine hair on her face
and body.

One stone, the whitest, she places in her mouth. The second
stone she takes
in her left hand, the third in her right, then she lies down on her bed.
So we are told. Because, of course, all this is hearsay. Some even say
the doors are never locked, that rice or burgers are daily provided.

Perfects are burnt, as men are, up in the mountains. Their bodies
are not seen.
But the house must be full of stones in drifts among the currant
bushes,
choking the well, piled in corners, on stairs — enough to break
your ankle —
white pyramids of round, sucked stones. They call it the *Pebble
House.*

SWALLOWING STONES

    Lena 1983

Anna is helping me
to make a basil garden
at the south end of the pasture.

She is picking up stones
to put in her pocket,
flints and pebbles bright from the night rain.

Three years old. Eyes russet.
Hair squirrel-red and flying
over bare cheek, still uncovered head.

Her pocket bulges and tears
and all the wet stones scatter.
Never mind, Anna, here's a basket.

She finds three small stones —
quartz, like sugarloaf —
and puts them in her mouth one by one.

They must feel cool and smooth
and pacify her tongue.
Spit them out, sweetheart, they'll harm you.

Wait a few years.
There'll be stones enough — huge,
crammed in your mouth to hold your tongue

and the great Stone Book
wedged over your heart.
It will lie, calling itself your soul.

Part Two, 1990 – 1998

BOYS ARE LIKE DIAMONDS, GIRLS ARE LIKE COTTON

Kor proverb

Lena Falada, January, 1990

And my Anna left below

while the diamond boys go up the stairs
the diamond boys go up one at a time
up the white steps studded and starred with glass
to the Salt Room, to the men's place.

And my Anna looking up

The diamond boys glitter at each other
They stand around the glass table
brilliant in the sunshine from the high panes
while the light changes all along the mountains.

My Anna at the bottom of the stairs

The staircase was wooden once, weathered
silvery grey. I remember how
it was replaced when the diamond boys
were born. Broken glass. Concrete.

Anna in her new apron

Anna's apron is more use than diamonds.
Such cloth is capable,
will clean and bandage wounds,
cover your cold body.

Anna with her brown scarf and her rag doll

Cotton is quiet and good, white fleece
from the black earth. Diamonds are only earth —
grown hard, fired, transfixed. It is wrong
to say they are precious. If you say so

people will believe it.
Anna may believe it.

MY FIRST VISIT TO THE SALT ROOM

>Anna Falada, April, 1990

This morning I found the helmet on the bed —
its weight on my feet like a large present.
My mother said *Anna Falada,*
you're ten years old. It's time.

She fastened it on with sharp twists of wire.
It was like wearing my own cupboard.
The clay smelled of the damp end of the cellar,
weighed down my neck. I fell over the stool
and breathed the same breath over and over.

I flung it off, ripping the wires,
cracked the side and spoiled the blue pattern.
My mother slapped my face.

Father's mother came in from the yard,
leaving her geraniums to tell me why.

>*Now, my cousin saw a woman's face*
high up at a window. He stripped naked,
drowned himself. Eighteen. The woman went unpunished
which was hard for us to bear.

My sister's stepson glimpsed a woman's face
when she lifted her helmet in the street.
He never worked afterwards, spoke to no one,
spent his days (I shouldn't tell you this) in self-abuse.
Again, a boy, sixteen.

And husbands need protection too. I remember
a man who killed his wife and children,
ruined, they said, by a smile from a bare face.

When I laughed, she beat me with the black skillet
and sent me to my father upstairs in the Salt Room.

His rooms were so full of light and air
I squinted and my face was snailed with tears.
But I could see from the window the river shining
and the mountains like a blue pattern on the sky.

He stood by the great stone salt box
and picked up a book
which he said was The Stone Book.
I had to touch the cover.

Little Anna, what is written is written.
No, you have nothing more to say.

But I said *Why is the Stone Book*
made of paper and cardboard
when I thought it was made of stone
and how can my face do wrong
when I'm not doing wrong?

I was beaten again with the black skillet
and Mother blamed my Aunt Lena
who has gone away. Where has she gone?

WHERE HAVE YOU GONE?

    Anna Falada, May 1990

When I ask they say *somewhere safe*
and Ren said *gone gardening*
and all my brothers laughed
except Fil who also loves you.

The tomatoes we put in have grown yellow flowers.
I water them every day and the peppers.
They haven't grown yet or the sweet-corn but
I can see little green hands in the soil.

You have plenty of gardening here, Aunt.
Come back. We can sit in the ruins
on the stone steps, the ones like water and silk.
We have so many good secrets.

I haven't told anyone. Father's Mother asked
what we talked about all the time and I said
Tomatoes and leeks and marjoram,
yellow peppers, courgettes and lavender,

sweet-corn, sunflowers and camomile... .
Then I saw she'd walked off.
I've hidden your box in the third house
by the broken fountain in the old city

where we used to go when it rained.
Mother said *What a pity she was*
always too clever. That was her problem.
She must have been talking about you.

I'll hide this letter too. I don't know where.
I'd talk to Fil but daren't. Now that he's twelve
he's one of the Salt-Bearers. You missed his Feast
and all the ceremony, his procession, the candles.

Aunt Lena, come back before the sweet-corn grows.

GRACE BEFORE THE MEAL

>Priest-Guardian Aguste, Chairman of the Council of the Elect, on the 25th December 1990 at the dinner of the Elect.

And the word was made spirit and dwelt amongst us
The Stone Book, Verse 320

My friends, my brothers, we know that in gross alien lands
men cram themselves with greasy meat on this holy day,

gorge on sweet suet, swill bright wine, grope their neighbours' wives,
belch, vomit, fall over, slide into a vile stupor.

We know that such men live in a sweaty dream of greed.
Flesh-worshippers, they snuffle round oven and brothel

until this holy day becomes the feast of Satan.
He stalks the world today and sees it is his own place

except in Kor. We keep the Christ birth day with fasting,
austere reverence, with deep prayer and quiet humility,

being wiser than the rest. Our Seer has taught us better,
making plain in *The Stone Book* the truth of Christ's birth day.

Our Seer was troubled by the pettiness of this life,
the sullen obstinacy of ordinary things

and wandered into the mountains to seek some respite,
easement in the plain geometry of barren rock.

Not a bush, not a leaf, not a flower, not a seed —
blessed emptiness — and high above the eagles' wings

at the top of a scree, an arete's thin edge,
God's voice spoke to him from the peak.

Consider Joseph, God-thinking man, carpenter,
patient mathematician, trimmer and planer of wood,

wise man of Nazareth, counsellor of neighbours:
how I came to him as sunlight through a glass window

and from his forehead sprang the spirit of Jesus Christ.
For we know, brothers and friends, that God has no mother

but was born from the mind of good Joseph, God-thinker,
to take on a child's semblance but never his body.

God did not enter here through the gate of flesh and blood
torn from a woman's body — that shameful heresy

which gross men celebrate today with feast and dancing.
But we know better and our meal is pure and seemly.

Therefore I call on Him whose voice echoed among the peaks,
echoed down gullies and silenced the cry of eagles,

to bless our humble bread and salt, to bless out dried fruit,
to bless us, mired in flesh, who look for Resurrection.

NAMELESS

    Anna Falada, June 1993:

In the morning when the airbus climbs
in a roaring curve to pass over the mountains
or, at twilight, steepens its descent,
then I can shout your name.

But I have lost you over and over —
you, your forbidden name, and now your room.
Father's bought a slave to do your work.
She sleeps on the floor beside the stored apples.

I sit in the camomile patch to talk to you
in the corner by the chestnut where you told me
you had buried my sisters. Five fine sons,
one daughter, then three baby girls, exposed

and given to the frost in three hard winters.
Can't we make them graves,
put up stones, give them names?
Call them my name if you like, you said,

but spare them headstones, Anna.
We live under stones. Let them
lie free in the earth, let their bare legs
sprawl easy, their faces go unmasked.

I think of three small worlds of bone
deep under the roots and scratchy stalks
of camomile, grown for Mother's migraine.
I don't believe that you are in the earth.

MUD FLOWERS

> Priest-Guardian Rickas, after evidence given by the Gabriels to the Elders in the Scrutiny into the deaths of fourteen women in Kor New City 6th June 1994.

She is the pearl in the oyster
forming slowly in the dark,
enclosed, protected.
The Stone Book, Verse 275.

The incident got out into the world
and was misreported by the foreign press
which ignorantly talked of mud masks.
They're wrong. Our helmets
are artefacts of culture from
a thousand year tradition, an indigenous
art form. Lacquered, they could line museum shelves.
Only some are plain mud. A few women of extreme
orthodoxy smear it on their face and let it dry
with the merest hint of decoration.
Some still gather tidal mud in the estuary
(because the Seer called women *mud flowers,*
soft creatures of the tides), and build their helmets
over wire frames, but when they dry they crumble
because of too much sand. Most use clay
from the river near Kor City. This is durable
and can be painted in an approved style. The wave
is the most popular design. Young women
have developed *papier mache,* which is lighter
and takes paint better, but many feel that helmets
made of paper can hardly be sincere.

The young men of the Gabriels are blameless.
This is the judgement of the elders of Kor City
after examination of the facts. The women
in the waters of the flooded cellar were unclothed —
they were bare-headed, their helmets gone.
The Gabriels requested most politely
that they put on their head gear
but *they screamed at us with bare nude faces*
using words they had no right to know
so we had to leave them there although
it upset us — all of it — but especially the nude faces.
And the women drowned. Sad, but God knows all
and has them in his keeping like pearls in a great shell.

FIL

> *"A heresy among a worse heresy": that was what Pope Pius IX called the teachings of Paven who was martyred in 1840 after a secret trial by the Committee of Doctrinal Enforcement in Kor. Paven's inclusive, quietist, perhaps even animist creed was spread by word of mouth and fiercely resented by the Kor establishment. It can be summed up in William Blake's phrase "Everything that lives is holy." Paven's teachings undermined the austere Aryanism of the Korish variety of Christianity. Paven was crucified upside down after the manner of St Peter. His last words, as he was led to the cross, were "There are many different ways of seeing things. This will be another view." His house in the remote and mountainous Kamiros province is still a shrine and attracts pilgrims despite the efforts of the Elders and militia. There is always a guard posted.*
> Dance, N. *Christian Cults*, New York, 1977, p 84

Narrative written by and circulated among the Paven cult after Fil's death in 1996.

On the third day he threw away his rifle
despite long months of murmuring and stroking
Kalashnikov, Kalashnikov.
But that long barrel and the bulge underneath —
incongruous, as he lay, fingers twined
in the sleek pelt of the grass.
He thought of rising and he did later
holding his rifle at arm's length.
He would fling it in the water.
But the stream nosed through the long grass
like a glistening animal.
He thought of his sister,
how she would like that water.
A bird he couldn't name spoke to him from the wood.

The shrine had no hiding place.
It was what it was — broken walls,
a fire-pit, flattened bracken in a corner,
a candle stub, a spent match.
It was a neat ruin, swept and garnished
with pots of marigolds.
One pot lay spilt from his first irritable day
and he picked it up, patted the earth back,
pinched off the pungent dead heads
as he'd seen his mother do. Women's work.
He imagined the old heretic watching the world
from this little valley hanging on the mountain
like a precarious shelf — Paven nursing his goats
and his peach trees, contemplating the sky
and the shadowy plain and the uplands.... .
Fil could almost see his own home. There
where the old forbidden city lay in ruins
gleaming in the sun. Just below that
and so close to the ruins that he used to watch
each dusk a smoke of bats swarm out of the city
and shudder. It didn't look so evil now.
The marigold smell was on his fingers still.

He found a green thicket in the shrine garden.
He could chuck his rifle there.
But it was like his grandmother's patch
where moths cling to the side of the wall
hidden behind the mint and rosemary.
This was mint too, gone wild, and full of purple flowers.
There was that old woman in the village
who sat among her herbs all afternoon
until he came back with the sheep and then
called out *Ready for your tea then, lad?*
That was all right really, not embarrassing...
She'd do something with this garden.

He scraped a hole in the thin, straggling woods-
under a young tree. It might be juniper.
He wrapped the rifle in his soldier's tunic
and shoved the ammo belt in too.
His brother would report him, probably.

Ren was a Gabriel now and a Commander
and held the Black Medal of the Seer
for shopping poor aunt Lena. But why shouldn't women
read and write? Who did it hurt? Did she deserve
forced labour in the rice-fields? But Ren was good.
The priest said so, called him *Fragment of Light*.
But what was good about shooting his collie, Samson
because he'd got too fond of it?
And then he tried to get the womenfolk
to wear the masks indoors for purity.
What a row that was! But Ren was good. The Gabriels
gave him a Skoda, for morality patrols
because he was such a marvel. Brand-new. White.

Clouds gathering and the darkness coming down:
the plain a shadow map remaking itself
with light. That dim cluster — Kamiros;
over there, Falan, and headlights from a car
point towards Korein. And unmistakable,
far to the east that orange glow
where foreigners were building Kor New City.
So many promises — malls, boulevards and traffic lights —
whatever these things were. *Gomorrah*
Ren called it but he would.
The candle was lit now in the shrine
and quiet people sitting there.
He'd go and join them at the accustomed time.

THE JOB OF APPREHENDING DARK SPIRITS

    Seminary Police Chief 1996

Down here are the holding bays,
six units and a larger room
for orientation. Don't slip there, brother.

Listen.
You have to understand
dark spirits to talk to them.
That's why we Seminary Police
are here. That's why the priests
train us for three years.
None of the Gabriel crowd
could do this job.

It's difficult — no dark societies
for us to weasel into.
They never meet,
they have no passwords,
but somehow they can recognise
each other. Weird. Solitary.

So, we collect them singly.
Employers surrender them.
Or families. Or we find one
curfew-breaking in the night.
They say they can't sleep.

Despair is both a sin and illegal.

Search. Locate. Interrogate.
That's our job. Then they're off

up to the mountain for
Re-education.

They're never chatty. Don't expect that.
Except one I picked up in the dark,
not even hiding, sitting below
the flood wall, on the steps,
where they turn to go into the river.
They're silted up and gone now.
He didn't try to run but talked at me
in that flat way they have.

Dark spirits are the only realists —
a scientist has proved it.

Yes, I punished him for that.
This is God's good universe, I shouted,
and you'll learn to enjoy it.
Don't set up your trivial, shivering,
 self-pitying personality
against God's goodness
and His chosen State of Kor.

Do you know what the bastard said?

It seems to me that life
is a dark cell, smeared with shit
and blood and I am lying there
being kicked by a fool.

I broke his jaw for that.

Despite my training
I find them hard to deal with.
You'll have to watch
they don't infect you.

Despair is somehow catching.
You'll need more than your gun.
No, we don't take women here.
Their families give them up
when they neglect their duties,
lie in bed all day and cry.
We ship them off in vanloads
to the marshes.

TIPTOE

> Anna reading Lena 1996. This is one of the poems found in Lena's box, hidden by Anna in the ruins of ancient Kor.

tiptoe
as if your bones
were honeycomb

go slow
as if your heart
beat out of tune

speak soft
as if your lungs
were full of dust

look down
as if the sun
would scald your eyes

keep still —
your breast and hair
are co-morbidities

hide your flesh, girl —
you have the symptoms but
the men are ill

IN THE BAR OF THE KOR NEW CITY MERIDIAN HOTEL

1. Charles Harding, July, 1998

I thought I'd got a visa for the ruins —
but maybe I got in someone else's car
or didn't pay the interpreter enough
or perhaps they needed a Brit to go along
with Barbara from Trade and Industry,
all frocked-up like a bee-keeper and sweating.
When I saw we were heading for the flatlands
instead of the mountains, I said *Hey,
let's see what happens,* but I didn't expect this.
I'd seen the lagoon from the air — mudflats
shining like a whatever-it-is guitar — but up close
it was desolation. Great set for sci-fi,
like some wet *Dune.* In the south, green stripes
where female prisoners are growing rice —
out of bounds for us, but it would make
a good opening shot, maybe letterboxed,
and then a jump cut to a face, masked.
We got to the site just as the sun was setting:
lagoon like a steel blade, marshes dazzling,
a line of women in those brown robes,
a brand new yellow crane with a muddy scoop.
The light was perfect for a panning shot,
a scrutinising, level sunlight. The convict
was held apart, her arms tied in front
so that her hands overlapped like an old lady's.
She stood quiet and straight as if she'd learned
her part and the other women were a Greek chorus
but silent, all their masks as still as exhibits.
Once at the Herodes Atticus ampitheatre
I saw — it may have been *The Bacchae* —

all the actors masked. Afterwards, faces seemed banal.
The scream was bad, though. It had seemed so like a play
but the scream was something else. If the convict screamed —
and I don't know that she did, then the whole thing
is... I don't know what I'm trying to say.
Anyway, somebody screamed and I felt bad.
Then she was lowered into the hole in the mud,
already filling with water. The women filed away
and the crane arm with the muddy scoop swung over.
Then the sun set. It would have made a good film
except for the scream. Which is still in my head.
Which is why I'm downing whiskies
and listening to Barbara prattle about helicopters.

2. Barbara Wells

It was a cock-up from the start.
Instead of talking to the Minister
I was shunted off to the coast
with that TV history guy in tight jeans.
Out of respect, I wore draperies
which were bloody hot. But Don,
the interpreter, still sat too close.
It was typical. The Americans
have grabbed the diamond franchise,
the French are building the new city,
the Germans are electrifying everything
and what happens to the Brits?
Instead of selling police expertise,
small arms and helicopters,
we're treated to an inhumation.
Imagine the *Daily Mail* headline —
Blair's Babe Views Execution
on Trade Mission Scandal
There'll be questions asked in the House.
I won't attempt any crypto-

colonial position, won't comment
on the incident. It would be inappropriate.
I could say I didn't look.
(I asked Don *What are they doing?*
What's her crime? He looked vague.
If she's here, she must be unchaste.)
I should have stopped looking.
I should have stopped looking.
Now this guy with the tight blue crotch
from Channel Four is vomiting
into what looks like a spittoon.
What a country. I ask you — a spittoon.

THE GABRIEL CHRIST

    Charles Harding, July 1998

Another trip out, this one more interesting
than the hydro-electric project with sea-water.
Why sea water I asked when every mountain
has waterfalls — some brothers to
Niagara? *The Bones of God,*
Bill said in the bar, *the mountains
are the Bones of God.* The Americans,
commissioned by the Elders,
are trying to build a road over the Salt Pass.
It needs one. That's where I was today.
My donkey was spectacularly unpleasant.
Some priests are furious though so work has stopped
and the hotel bar is full of bored Americans
cursing the government.
I'm not Current Affairs. I've nothing to say
except I wish they'd sent Michael Palin
whom donkeys seem to like. I ache —
my bones, the donkey's bones, the bones of God...
Barbara stayed behind to nurse her vodka habit
but women are forbidden anyway.

The Salt Pass starts off with tarmac and beer stalls
but soon deteriorates. Sky, rock and water —
boulders big as a car, tumbling scree, cliffs closing in
until we reached a crevice in black rock.
It was like toiling upward into a cave
with intermittent shafts of grey light.
Ten hours on an irritable donkey
but there's a project in it.
After a rocky switchback ride,
we found on the other side

nothing but desert, a great grey plain
completely empty.

There was a camp of Gabriels at the mouth of the pass
— those young guys in black — the armed youth movement
who help the police. Then Don told me
about the Forty Days: how every man in Kor
has to spend forty days out in the desert
in honour of the Great Lord Christ.
But a man can spin it out all his life.
A few hours here or there, it soon adds up.
Don's wilderness trip is measured out
in six-hour slots. Already he's on number seventy two.
He strolls out and lies behind a rock
until it's time to stagger back again.
A very few decide on total imitation —
forty days, no food, no drink, no shelter.
(But what do they expect – angels
with food parcels or caterer ravens?)
It's quite a cool thing among the Gabriels
who field a saint a year. Interesting.
I could pitch this quite well. A PTC,
maybe more of a reflective piece.
But I don't know yet about the ruined city.
I'll make the world sit up if I can get there,
especially if I meet up with that contact
mentioned in Changeling's letters.

We stayed all night watching the Gabriels drink
and warming ourselves tactfully at their fire.
I haven't seen many drunks in Kor
but did last night. *They are so good,*
Don said, *they can do anything.*
For a whole month before his trip,
The Gabriel Christ has access
to the women prisoners.

He can have any one of them or all.
The priest gives him a wad of marriage lines
and he fills in the names. It's quite legal.
If the Gabriels hear of a girl's beauty
they make sure she's arrested.
The cells are full of lovelies for the Gabriels.

I said nothing. I'm not Current Affairs,
but I didn't like the grin on Don's face
(trivial little guy) so turned away and ate
my bacon and avocado sandwich
and waited for the morning. Thick frost,
stars like icicles, donkeys shifting,
their hooves clattering on the rocks,
the steady chugging of whisky from the boys
who, toward dawn, began a steady chanting.
Long Live Death, Don translated,
Long Live Death.

Then, the quiet one in the ill-fitting uniform
got up and walked away. No fuss. No speeches.
Long Live Death. And the sun rising,
the sky a polished metal shield,
his shadow stretching back towards us.
That shot would make a good top for the piece.
We watched him, saw his arm move —
then we were face down, covered in dirt
and the donkeys screaming. Grenade?
That's how the Gabriels worship God
with thunder in the desert. He'll have dynamite as well
and every dawn will set off an explosion
until.... Don shrugged, *he dies,* I said.
There's something fine about that.

The Gabriels were chanting something else,
no longer *Long Live Death*.
His name, Don said, *they're honouring Falada.*
But that's the name I'm looking for,
Falada, the person who might help me
in the ruins. It couldn't be that skinny lad,
a Lowry figure, now a mile away.
Or could it? Don stopped me, horrified.
You can't go in there. That's the Mind of God.

THE ANGEL RENDEZVOUS

Blessed are the righteous for they shall see God.
The Stone Book, Verse 3

Ren Falada, July, 1998

1 He has spent his life making for this horizon

runrun youcan run now forever yourfeetaskeenasfuck get away run
thisisyourreal life all your life this rock this sand long time
running no one else no weak father no waterweak father no brother
this salt this sky this coming here running to the angel
this dry this pure no whores no sluts no mudstupid mother
no whoring sister loose in the fields you're running now

angel holds your hand hold it hard keep hold angel of the fire
make a blessed noise for the angel bang bang you're dead
and another grenade all for God run wiped out whores for God
all the little wives foul but clean now washed in blood laid out
on the floor running to the sun leaping to the fiery angel

angel come out of the sun take me up burn me through burn me out
take me in fire clean me in fire take me to the sun the eye
of the sun the sun is an eye the eye of God God's eye
I will see God in that ecstasy I will see God

God's eye on the horizon

no not the dark I finished all the little wives for you
washed in blood for the angel to take me I crept up on my brother
in the night not the dark the dark is too dark they lay there
oozing filth leaking sin rock sand salt sky dark

2 *The coming of night purifies him*

three clouds shining   thunder   silence   and now the dark
and the blow of the cold

no angel

where is the promised angel red-winged they said striding
out of the sun

God is testing me

forgive my most grievous fault

dark is strong   make my soul strong   the strong soul sees God

the desert's will   and the will of the dark   God's will

 rock sand salt sky   pure   I am pure

desert wiped dark by God's hand

night wind is the power of God   everything erased   unmade

no tracks no marks no filthy life

God's hand on my head   watch   keep awake watch the dark
temptation in the water bottle   pour it away into the dark
hear it gurgle hear it splash into the sand   bury the bottle
no water bottle   God's test   my brother on the heretic hill

make a blessed noise for God   bang bang he's dead   dust
clouds of dry dust and the dark

3 He wakes knowing someone has entered his enormous room

fucking moon spying moon scrambling up the sky   my mother
clambering up the stairs spy moon sailing along
not a care in the world   pagan fucking moon
star with blue light going up beside
like a little kid with a torch

>His mother had shown him the moon
>in the well once — was he four? —
>then laughed and pointed upwards.
>He'd laughed too......

God

Knifewhere'stheknife forgive my fault stabinthethigh
forgive my fault stabinthethigh

quickunbuttontheholster   forgive my most grievous fault
firethepistolfire into the sky shoot the white slug moon
fat spider moon the pagan fucking moon shoot it shoot
again and again

blood trickles black in the moonlight   forgive

4 He is the voice of one crying in the wilderness

sun returns a gong a swung gong in the sky gong noise   brazen
gong noise

a wandering fire to serve God with noise how many grenades left

Bang bang they're all dead

dust but the gong is louder

tongue a brass bell crowding the mouth

what I've done for you great lord God   what I've done

let the angel come   send the fiery angel

here's the chocolate bar   the gang hid it under the last grenade
a Mars bar oozing and melting dripping the warm chocolate smell
the last temptation

how easy it is to throw it away
thunder   make thunder
Bang bang she's dead

was that an answer
almost an answer
maybe an answer

not a drop of hated water
not a shovel of earth
not a flower
nothing here trivial
nothing compassionate

rock sand salt sky

Anna is walking beside you and you scream at her to put on her mask
but she looks at you with her scarred face and with her bleeding
fingers pulls off her coverall and you scream again
because her breasts are torn and bleeding and she paints her face
with blood to make a mask
get out you scream   *get out*
but she's a child now very little   two or three years old
Aunt Lena she says *Aunt Lena*

5 Make straight the way of the Lord

the fiery angel will rush towards you with thunder and fire
out of the molten doorway of the sun and swoop down on you
annihilating you pure as a flame pure as air   you will see God

didn't I do what Abraham couldn't do   execute my own kin
didn't I go behind him   up on the heretic's hill
when he knelt in the shrine   didn't I put a pistol to his neck
didn't I blow him away   apostate   cursed of God   it was best
that I should do it   he'd gone rotten   dishonoured God

your feet move
but you are becoming spirit
spirit
abstraction
erasure

foul body dropping away
infected polluted full of blood and shit
dropping away

do your feet move

all the little wives laid dead on the floor
I did them a favour   they were flies and filth

6 The dead do not go away

who is this walking towards you through the glare and the shimmer
of the rock and the sand and the salt and the sky

walking softly towards you

making no sound on the sharp pebbles

walking towards you as if he were your brother

as if he were your brother coming to ask for a football
or a game of tag

Fil is walking towards you

he is between you and the sun so that his shadow reaches out
to touch you

7 God my God, why have you forsaken me

sand

        rock

 salt

                      sky

8 Death is a dry place

AT THE MINISTRY

    Barbara Wells, August, 1998

Fuck off, Charles, this is the wrong
time for anything like that.
I can't take this country —
don't tell me anything more
about it.

If I tell you why, you'll put it in
some documentary about New Labour —
their ignorance of foreign affairs
their Pollyanna optimism.
It's true, though.

They shouldn't have sent me here.
But why the fuck not? I'm the best.
But, Christ, the day I've had!
Talked over and around, overlooked, ignored.
Ostracised. Is that the word?

No, it was more like a small
annihilation. I proposed the contract
but the Minister spoke only to my aide,
junior but male — that irritating Hugo —
he talked all round me,

    never looked at me. My voice shrivelled
    up and died in that damn marble room.
    It was much worse that I can say.
    Weirdest thing — it was like being stared at
    by blind people.

And this was the big deal. This
was what I came for. A shitty half hour
of invisibility. I was there, wasn't I?
I'm tough — but not to be looked at,
not to be there... I was bloody there.

Don't you dare tell anyone of this.
I've fixed Hugo. I know stuff about him
his mother wouldn't like to hear about.
She's a religious nut, like everyone here.
God-botherer, sex-hater.

My legs were wobbly and I kept thinking —
I can see why — of a time in the salt marshes
walking on boggy wetlands near the sea
when the ground tipped under my feet
like a huge see-saw.

I keep thinking of that and how my body
panicked. Then I think of Hugo's face,
so smug and tactful. Fuck this awful place.
The driver took us back through the chaos
of this hellish city and we stopped

among the petrol stinks and shouts
and filthy great holes and huge
sky-scraper cranes. A horse was loose
among the lorries. We were stuck for hours
outside a new and shining hospital.

That place, the interpreter said,
is for the *ladymen*. Instead
of hanging, they can change their sex
at the government's expense.
I think he said that.

Choose between a public execution
and a forced sex change. Do gay men
want to be women? I don't think so.
I know my brother doesn't. And Hugo
lost his smug look immediately.

A great red sign outside the hospital
clarified the situation. It translated
MAN OR WOMAN: NO OTHER OPTION.
But what surgery do they have for women —
these trailing figures in brown robes

and masks, never alone, always in threes and fours
with an attendant male — guard or guardian?
I used to think of cultural differences
but now I think the mask covers a blankness
all features excised by the government.

IN PRAISE OF RUINS

    Charles Harding, August, 1998

God, Barbara, you're a politician.
You can't afford to get political.
Lighten up — you're not some dungareed
grim crone from the seventies.
As you said on the plane — we must respect
all cultural differences. You said it twice.
You're pissed off about the Minister.
But that's cultural too, and the women
and the gay men — all deeply cultural
and nothing to do with us. And who are we
to judge? We have pornography and pole-dancing.
You've got what you want — the contract.
Forget the rest. Think about people
who really need your help. Think about me.

But you're so right about this hideous city:
Korish post-modernist malls and ziggurats
hurt the eyeballs. Do what I do
when I see something ghastly — imagine it in ruins.
Ruins are dignified. That smug hospital
becomes a nest of concrete stumps,
three spears of glass catching the sun,
metal spars like Giacometti lines,
elongated, fragile, reduced to anxious gesture... .
Who are you calling arse-hole? Listen to me.
I've had a bad time too down in the waterless desert.
This isn't Godalming or Guildford. So think
of something else. And why not ruins?

When I was a kid, I discovered a ruin —
an ancient chapel lost in rhododendrons,

Medieval, Gothic — I could tell
by the wonderful curve of the window.
I sketched it, counted all the stones
and reported my findings to the catering manager
of the Gunnersbury Park Tearooms.
Of course he said they knew about it,
pointed it out on some map.
And it wasn't even a proper ruin.
They'd built it like that in the eighteenth century.
Yes, I suppose it was funny.
But after that I made ruins everywhere:
St Paul's wrecked to an egg cup with a splintered shell;
Westminster honed down to the Old Man of Hoy;
my parents' house a wall of shallow
chimney breasts, a litter of Spode china.
Great fun. When I was sacked from the BBC
you should have seen the mess I made of it —
in my own head of course. But that fake ruin
in a west London park made me what I am:
a *ruin-bibber*, someone called it. That's why
I'm here. And why I need your help.

Now that Kor has stopped doing an Albania,
the place is getting busy. Soon
there'll be camera crews and TV archaeologists.
No, I'm not paranoid. Ancient Kor is unexplored.
That old city up in the hills could be El Dorado,
King Solomon's Mines, Shangri La.
And I've got the visa now. Don and I start tomorrow.
But we need you. We may have to talk to women.
Well, what else will you do?
You could sit here swilling gin and tonic
or you could come with us and see something
extraordinary. No, I won't tell you now
but I'll let you read some notes from the one
English guy who's been up there — Frank Changeling —

twenty years back when Kor had a friendly spell
which soon fizzled out. He got back to the UK
but never returned to Kor. His widow gave me his letters
because I'm on TV. Don's found a Landrover
and we're off tomorrow. Come with us.
You'll love ruins by moonlight.
Did you know the loudest echo in the world
is in the Colisseum?

BUTCHER

    Anna reading Lena 1998 (from a manuscript found in Lena's box)

the butcher came to our home
with his big scissors and his knife
and four aunts to hold me down
he sliced me and trimmed me
all the place between my legs
carved out, scraped to the bone

UP COUNTRY

    Barbara Wells, August, 1998

(i)

If anyone had asked, I would have said
yes I quite like them — sunflowers.
They have a bashed-up bruiser look;
surly, top-heavy, they glower at you
and don't pretend, like pansies, that they like you.
But to travel through miles and miles
of sunflowers on a track made by ox carts
with two men I detest! My self-esteem
must have been more damaged
than I realised to let me in for this.

There's something Charles isn't telling me.
I've known it all along. He's got rid of the driver
and suddenly produced a video camera,
explained it all to Don, so Don is now
driver, interpreter and camera-man
while Charles is trying to charm me
but will fail. He thinks he's Indiana Jones
even in his Tilley hat and long shorts.
Christ, I want to be in my own flat, quite alone,
with a glass of Bollinger, some retro music.

Yellow is the vilest colour. It's like crawling
through incandescent custard powder.
God help these poor women, all togged-up
in mask and browns, working in the fields.
Don pointed to them, takes great pleasure
in filling me in on every detail
of how this place behaves to women.

I don't respond. That's what he wants.
But after the House of Commons bar,
I can cope with his misogyny.

(ii)

It's a bit like Rumania, I think,
flat plains and then a steady rise
towards the mountains. Maize fields now.
Still yellow. Fewer villages but
little boys who must live under rocks
rise up from nowhere to annoy us.
Trabb's boy, I thought of, when I first saw them
even after their shower of stones
but Charles and Don got rattled
and begged me to wrap up, so now
I'm swathed like Rider Haggard's She.

Don is going to film that Carter moment,
Charles says, when he discovers
whatever he's going to discover.
Who? I asked.
    When they knocked through
to the tomb and Howard Carter whispered
'Wonderful things'.
    What did he find?
He saw the various gleams of gold,
the quiet shadows of exquisite furniture,
the jewel-encrusted tomb of a boy-king... .
OK. I get the picture. You're a grave-robber?
Certainly not, he said and gave me Changeling's letters.

(iii)

I shouldn't be here, I really shouldn't be here.
Frank Changeling's made me sure of that.
He was crazy to come here too.
But to map the ruins with a Korish woman!
No wonder he was chucked out.
Did he think this was Cambridge? What happened
to her I wonder? And then to find it
or rather the woman found it, led him to it –
the *wonderful thing* that Charles is after now.
I can't be party to this cultural raiding
because that's what it is and there'll be hell to pay
back in the Commons if and when it gets out.

But *wonderful thing* it is —
even in these fading Polaroids, the exquisite
girl, utterly nude with such an air
of cheek. Insouciance is probably the word.
Her arms akimbo (such skinny little elbows),
she's slightly leaning back, with one leg
forward, knee bent. Her snub-nosed head cocked
to one side, short hair in close ridges,
expression insolent — d*on't mess with me
but aren't I great* — is what she's saying.
And she is. Slim, utterly bare,
her vulva plump and prominent,
she's probably sixteen. *Bronze*
says the letter, *age and provenance unknown*.
But who in Kor made this?

PATRIARCH

    Jon Falada 1998

Water, then wine. Now bread and salt and blessings,
travellers, for honouring me, a stranger,
with your visit. God leads the wanderer.

Changeling? I would prefer a better name
with gentler memories. He cost us pain
and money, nearly had my sister killed.

I had to pay the Gabriels all my fleece cash
and promise them my eldest son. They went
without her, left her breath but little else.

And so my troubles started. God has marked me,
friends, with his attention, like Job
in the old book. I still trust His mercy.

But Ren, the marvellous boy, is gone;
Fil lost to me and God; Lena removed
and my poor wife dead in the wicked city.

The Seer abjured us to avoid all cities,
places of vice and singing — dancing even.
Stick to the goat paths, he said. God is there.

God is angry and I suffer, but His will
be done. I can't help you, gentlemen.
Lena is gone who knew the ruins

although they are forbidden. I can take you
to the first stone. I prefer my garden,
my mother's flowers and the sound of insects

where I can sit and read the old book,
quite superseded now but not forbidden,
and know the cricket's song to be a burden

and my sons will not return to me,
for all our days are but sorrows
and the mourners go about the streets.

GHOST

Barbara Wells, August, 1998

It was the gentlest sound: a squirrel
leaping from a branch, an acorn
falling in long grass. I hardly heard it
there at the Falada farm. I was left
like a parcel in the car, to watch
the men ascend that special staircase,
enter the upper room.

Restricted Territories —
badlands, bandit country,
so the police said at the checkpoint,
rebels in the mountains, cult-followers,
heretics. I stayed where I was.

Then again, the tap of a moth on glass.
JESUS, what a shock, a brown mud mask
pressed to the window. I smiled,
hoping it was a woman. But
how do you talk to a mask?
She took it off. I'd never seen that before.
She was only a kid, sixteen, seventeen,
pretty except for the red scar on her cheek.
She beckoned to me, gestured towards
the mountains. *No thanks,* I mouthed,
I'm staying here and shook my head.
She was frightened, glanced at the house.
Who was she? Then she thrust a photograph
against the glass.

        God, that statue again
but from another angle, clearer now.

The wonderful thing. Was one of her arms raised?
(I'd thought they were both akimbo.)
But such a sense of movement! Yes
She was going to dance — for herself,
just for her own pleasure.
I scrambled out of the car and followed the scarred girl.

A couple of miles of rough pasture,
and rising ground, the mountain wind against us,
gusting about her robes and tangling my daft veil.
I took it off and looked back. Charles and Don
were stick men scurrying about the car.
I'd find the statue first, make sure Charles
didn't steal it. Art should be left *in situ*.
I told myself this but I wanted the wonderful
thing like I wanted my first boy-friend,
like I wanted the moon.

Then, from the brow of the hill, I saw the famous city.
To tell the truth, I'm not too keen on ruins.
What are they for? They make me think of graveyards
and that's what they really are. From above
those acres of stone walls reminded me
of one of those hand-held children's games
where you guide a ball through obstacles.
But the kid was down there, threading the streets
like the ball itself and I ran down after.
(Who was she? She couldn't be Changeling's guide.)

If the Pere Lachaise cemetery in Paris —
everything, tombs and all —
had swollen up a hundred times
and been dumped on these mountains... .
That's what it was like. Those ornate
little houses for the dead where souls
can crouch in the rain: here they were —

huge and frightening and hardly touched
by time and weather. Even I could see
it was a well-preserved necropolis.

The kid back in her mask
was waiting for me by a great square tank
once full of water. The walls were
carved with flowers, quite un-stylized.
I thought I recognised some cranesbill.
But she was off again, clambering
steps, her brown robes flapping,
up to a house or temple, less florid
than the rest. Was this the place?

ANCIENT KOR

    Charles Harding, August 1998

Marble sometimes, granite mostly —
white, like Macchu Picchu. God,
look at it — a colonnade
with arches still intact.
Hardly broken. Temples —
they must be — raised on solid
blocks of masonry. And look —
magnificent, extraordinary
staircase. Columns five deep.
Trapezoidal doorways
with unmortared stones.
Elaboration on that
column base — fruit and flowers
and birds and vine leaves and
a ring of rams' heads... .

Are you getting all this, Don?
Film those ornamental lintels.
We need details. They always sell.
And the statue will persuade the world
this is a heritage site.
We haven't got much time but
Burckhardt only had a day
and he discovered Petra.
Layard of Nineveh, Schleimann of Troy,
and soon — Harding of Kor... .

Shit, this is the Sacred Way —
must be — a triumphal avenue
paved and wide and shining
with benches, columns, fountains —

I think that rubble is a fountain.
What little town by river or seashore
Or mountain-built with peaceful citadel
Is emptied of its folk this pious morn?
Dame Judi's voice maybe or a silent tracking
up this avenue? Or perhaps some Schubert?

Look there — a compound of stone animals
and trees are growing through them.
A turtle with an oak on its back —
a marketing opportunity, I'd say.
Dendrofication is not widespread
however. I suspect gardening.
Barbara's guide — who must be the famous
Lena (I knew that old guy lied
when I saw two women on the hill)
— must come here often and bring
all her friends. Will I have to wrest
that statue from a cult?

    No, she must
be by herself. This place is cursed,
forbidden ten times over. They all
 went away and left it.
And little town, thy streets for evermore
Will silent be; and not a soul to tell
Why thou art desolate, can e'er return.
What a story. What a TV series.
And that statue — goddess, whatever it is,
that'll front the book with turtle
on the back cover.

    There she is —
Barbara, doing a Niobe, trailing veils
and posing on the staircase to a temple
or very small palace. Is that

a lustral bath? She's pointing
to the temple. Don, let's go.
Never mind the carvings. We want
the statue. It must be in here.

THE DANCING GIRL

Barbara Wells, August, 1998

I went back in when I heard him shouting
although I didn't want to see it again.
Barbarians, he was screaming, *bloody peasants.*

The girl was slowly gathering scattered fragments:
bronze bones gleams of twisted metal
a broken hand fingering the dust

nothing whole   a skinny elbow fractured
an arm smashed to metal pulp
bronze limbs hacked and stamped hard down

the head beaten in with a rifle butt
or axe   battered   destroyed   four bronze bangles
stamped flat   a hand with all the fingers twisted off

torso ravaged   boot marks on the belly
vulva kicked in   axe buried in the breasts.
This erasure must have taken hours.

Don was gaping round. Charles, head in hands,
sat on the edge of the low dais, muttering.
Fucking barbarians, appalling filthy, yobbish ignorance....

And the red words everywhere, painted huge
on walls and floor. It turned that quiet room
into a London subway. There should have been

fast food cartons, needles on the floor,
a litter of tramp trash to go with the graffiti —
three red letters sprayed on every surface

REN REN REN REN REN REN
REN REN REN REN REN REN
I don't know what REN is but its brutality

was clear. It meant that nothing beautiful
or good or clever could ever last
but bigotry and hate would kill it.

I felt like crying, stooped to a gleam of bronze
and found a tiny finger, joints and nail intact
and took it to the girl, still gathering every splinter.

Charles flounced out and Don followed
thrusting the camera at me.
Should I go? I wanted to stay.

I wanted to stay with the girl
whoever she was. I looked
at where her face should be and smiled.

She took off her mask and smiled back,
gestured towards the camera, began to speak.
That's how I came to film the sequence.

It's famous now. Do I need
to describe again that ghastly striptease,
drab garments falling to the floor,

the revelation of that battered body?
Slashed face, the suppurating breast wound,
discolorations of a hundred bruises,

between the legs the livid scar tissue
like ancient burning, and evidence
of recent trauma — torn flesh, the dribble of new blood.

She laughed but I was stricken, horrified
by the story written on her body
and that my silence could imply consent.

WHAT SHE SAID

    Anna Falada, August, 1998

Lena called her *Bronze Anna*
or *Long Ago Anna*
or *Tomorrow Anna*
I call her *Anna*
which is my name too

I'll still talk to her
She's in my head
You have to talk to someone
in your head
I talk to Lena too

and she's deep now
asleep, tucked up in the mud
taken by the wetlands
moving with the slow tides
covering the mudflats

Lena isn't surprised
She knew what would happen
to the Bronze Anna if anyone found her
anyone like Ren found her
I hoped you could protect her

It's a clean room and the light is good
when I open the shutter — look,
Lena made this shutter — you can see
the sky with its great hem of mountains
and all over my mysterious Kor

This is where I go to in my head
It's always there no matter what happens
When three men dishonoured me
in the new city after my mother died
I kept my thoughts on this place

I counted every house climbed each stair
And in prison too when I was convicted
I kept my thoughts on this place
dreamed of the mist faltering
down the mountain

creeping through the empty streets
blotting everything out
even the Gabriels when they came
to punish the women for unchastity
by raping us

Ren came and slashed my face
with the knife our father gave him
at his Salt Ceremony
It's hard to be good he said *and pretty
but this will make you wear your mask*

I went to this place in my head
sat on the *reading cushions* (we called them)
where she taught me to read and write
and talk about more things than we could
in my father's house or in the rest of Kor

Always there was Bronze Anna
and we talked to her too
Lena said *Not every girl in the world
has her sex sheared away with a knife
Not every girl hurts when she passes water*

*or walks too far or squats down suddenly
or has to be cut open when she marries
sewn up again when she's given birth
When you think of men* Lena said
You have to think of knives

Knives and stones But my father
isn't like the men who took me
when my mother died and kicked me
tore my stitches and bit my breasts
in the waste land beyond the car park

Look, this is what they did to me —
these wounds are not healing.
And Ren is wicked whatever people say
I heard him in the next cell
with the blonde girl who disappeared

What is there in Nature, Lena asked
*that makes these stone hearts —
stone hearts and stone words?
Who makes us swallow stones
and pelts us with stone words?*

They cut my hair back into the scalp
in prison They called it *whore's hair*
It's growing slowly into clumps
I would like it long again and flowing
tangled by the wind or bouncing in a plait

I would like to walk in the hills
with the sun and the wind on my bare face
I would like to work among the sweet-corn
with my arms and legs free of the coverall
free of the gloves and thick stockings

I would like to climb the steps to the ruins
without a burning pain between my legs
I would like to walk through a street
or out of a hospital without fear
of the men with stone hearts and knives

I would like to sit in the evening
and read a book in my grandmother's garden
I would like to go to a library or school
talk loudly argue with people
say what I think tell them about Lena

I would like to laugh out loud
I would like to run I would like to marry
(no one will marry me now)
I would like to have ten daughters
I would teach them all to read

I would like to take my clothes off
and let the air touch my grey body
I would like to wear bangles
and a pink dress I would like to dance
I would like to dance